© Félicity Vincent (Spoonful of Felicity) 2024

SEASONAL MOOD FOOD

EASY EVERYDAY RECIPES & FUN FACTS

VOL. 1 - AUTUMN

Fill your week with wholesome seasonal dishes to eat 30+ plants a week and improve your mental well-being.

FELICITY VINCENT

I dedicate this book to my best friend who happens to also be my mother, thank you for everything.

Félicity Vincent
Spoonful of Felicity on behalf of MoodMoves Ltd
https://spoonfulfelicity.com/

INTRODUCTION

I might shock you: green vegetables make you happier. I know, my 5 year old nephew would definitely be the first to refute this too!
But let's take a step back: we are all told that to live a healthier life and prevent disease we should exercise regularly and eat 5 fruit/veg a day. And yes, that's important, but what is health? It's not only about our heart, or how much fat we have, it's also about our mental health. And it turns out this is also affected by what we eat.

Coffee is high in caffeine. Therefore, drinking coffee makes you feel more awake, that's pretty obvious! But, many other unsuspected foods also have a big impact: did you know that cabbage is high in folate which supports the production of serotonin and therefore a feeling of happiness and serenity? Similarly, egg is rich in tryptophan which is a precursor of serotonin. And spinach is a good source of Vitamin C which allows our body to produce noradrenaline, the hormone best known for 'runner's high'.
Every season brings its own wonderful ingredients full of nutrients with their own special unique compounds to impact not only our body's health, but by helping us to function properly they also allow us to regulate our moods!

Let's get one thing straight. I'm not trying to say that eating more plants can replace therapy! You don't just need to eat a whole cucumber and the grey clouds float away... As someone who suffers from anxiety and low mood, I can't

recommend enough seeking medical advice. But eating a balanced diet full of plants and gut friendly foods is another tool to have in the arsenal which shouldn't be overlooked! Think of it as the first building block you can take control of.
In this book, I hope to show how food impacts our mood and give you the tools and recipes for everyday, so each fun fact and nudge brings you closer to happier eating. I've started with the Autumn volume of the series, as we all know that the shorter days and lack of light can really affect our moods and I believe this recipe book can help!

Good mood food starts with meals everyone RAVES about!

Rainbow - Try to eat the rainbow over a week and if possible every day;
Allow everything - Forbidden foods are often counterproductive;
Variety - Scientific research shows we should aim for over 30 different plants a week;
Every meal - Try to include plants in every meal you eat;
Seasonality - Try to eat seasonally.

Why should I eat the rainbow?

One of my favourite thing about fruit and veg is their beautiful range of colours. We eat with our eyes first after all! And that's actually why fruit is so colourful, it has evolved with the strategy to get eaten so seeds can be dispersed, so plants have made themselves attractive to our greedy eyes. They achieve this through pigments, and these can be very specific for each plant, for instance the red in peppers is made from a unique blend of carotenoids, which is different to the red of tomatoes. These pigments also have many health benefits, from red lycopene maintaining skin health and protecting from UV damage, to green chlorophyll reducing oxidation by free radicals and protecting brain cells. That's one of the reasons it's essential to get a bit of every colour in the diet.

Why allow everything?

These are all principles to keep in mind, not rules, food should still be enjoyable and something to look forward to as we have to eat 3 times a day! Forbidden foods (except for allergies of course!) are most often counterproductive, creating a bad relationship with food. Like all relationships, the key is happy compromise! Eating a bit of everything, with balance. Even cake has its benefits, for one it makes us happy!

Why should I eat a variety of different plants every week?

A healthy microbiome is also key to better health and mood management. Your microbiome is the collection of bacteria living in your gut, most of which are very friendly and beneficial. Not a lot of research had been done into our microbiome's role until recent years, but it has now been shown to have a big impact on our health and most notably brain health. A gut brain axis allows for communication between the two organs and it seems a happy gut = a happy brain. To develop a healthy microbiome, scientists first recommend eating a lot of prebiotics, aka food for our gut bacteria, aka fibre; and probiotics, aka live bacteria, aka fermented foods. So to achieve a healthy diversity of bacteria, it's recommended to eat over 30 different plants a week.

How do I count how many different plants I'm eating?

I've indicated the number of plants in each dish with a little apple symbol. Although these may repeat themselves my proposed menus ensure you definitely get 30 different ones each week.

If you want to count how many plants are in your meals, here are the rules:

- 1 plant = 1 point, but it can't be repeated twice;
- 2 different coloured plants = 2 points (green and red peppers);
- Plants = vegetables, fruits, legumes, nuts and seeds, whole grains;
- Frozen, tinned and dried also count but juices don't;
- Vegetable stock = 0.5 points;
- Dried herbs, spices, coffee, tea, garlic and extra virgin olive oil (EVOO) = 0.25 points.

How is eating seasonally better for my physical and mental wellbeing?

The benefits are 3-fold:
1. Vegetables lose nutrients as they get picked, transported, left to ripen, or wait on shelves. Eating seasonally (or frozen while in season) is one way to ensure maximum nutrients in the ingredients.
2. They are cheaper and therefore it's easier to include more of them.
3. It's an easy way to vary what you eat if you follow the seasons rather than eating the same plants all year round. Nature's meal planner if you will!

EXAMPLE WEEK MENUS

Sounds too complicated and fussy? Try using the menus I propose for the next 2 weeks. This should help you get your head around it and discover lots of easy delicious meals, full of plants! I find being organised enough to bring a healthy breakfast and lunch into work a sure mood booster too! Delicious breakfast, lunch and easy dinner sorted.

WEEK 1

	MONDAY	TUESDAY	WED	THURSDAY	FRIDAY
Brekky	Berry Parfait Overnight Oats	Berry Parfait Overnight Oats	Berry Parfait Overnight Oats	Berry Parfait Overnight Oats	
Lunch	Autumn Lunch Box	Autumn Lunch Box	Parsley Pesto Pasta	Chickpea Harissa Stew	Chicken Pie
Dinner	Miso Bowls	Parsley Pesto Pasta	Chickpea Harissa Stew	Chicken Pie	

WEEK 2

	MONDAY	TUESDAY	WED	THURSDAY	FRIDAY
Brekky	Apple Crumble Porridge	Apple Crumble Porridge	Apple Crumble Porridge	Apple Crumble Porridge	Apple Crumble Porridge
Lunch	Autumn Lunch Box	5-Bean Burrito Bowl	Autumn Lunch Box	5-Bean Quesadilla	Autumn Chicken Traybake
Dinner	5-Bean Burrito Bowl	Butternut Squash Orzo	5-Bean Quesadilla	Autumn Chicken Traybake	

SHOPPING LISTS

The quantities in this book are based on cooking for 2 people; adjust by halving for 1, multiplying by 2 for a family of 4 etc. Some ingredients overlap between both weeks for less waste, and the spices and stock cubes will last for months to be used in future recipes.

SUNDAY PREP:

These recipes require a bit of prep in order to make an easy quick meal during the week.

- Apple Crumble Porridge
- Berry Parfait Overnight Oats
- Autumn Lunch Box
- 5 Bean Chilli
- Miso Tofu and Aubergine Bowls

WEEK 1

2 aubergines
2 small sweet potatoes
200g potatoes
2 spring onions
1/2 celeriac
1 leek
1 seasonal cabbage
300g button mushrooms
1/2 butternut squash
1 pepper
1 carrot
1 pear
Spinach or lettuce leaves
30g rocket
3 red onions
5g ginger
7 garlic cloves
125g parsley
8g coriander
2 lemons
1 lime
570mL milk of choice
10 Tbs strained live yogurt
70g grana padano cheese
2 chicken breasts
250g tofu
5 sheets of filo pastry
120g oats
100g basmati rice
360g pasta
25g plain flour
2 tins of chickpeas
1 tin of green lentils

1 tin of tomatoes
4 Tbs chia seeds
30g mixed seeds
5g sesame seeds
30g walnuts or almonds
80g almonds
20g flaked/whole almonds
35g dried apricots (approx 5)
2 Tbs honey
2 tsp sugar
4 Tbs tahini
2 Tbs white miso paste
2 tsp harissa paste
2 tsp dijon mustard
3 Tbs soy sauce
1 vegetable stock cube
120mL EVOO
4 Tbs vegetable oil
2 tsp balsamic vinegar
4 Tbs apple cider vinegar
3 Tbs ras-el-hanout
4 tsp ground cumin
2 tsp ground cinnamon
Sea salt
Black pepper
320g frozen mixed berries
100g frozen broccoli
80g frozen peas

WEEK 2

1 cabbage
1 aubergine
1 butternut squash
3 carrots
2 celery sticks
3 red peppers
1/3 cucumber
1 celeriac
170g (approx) button mushrooms
240g (approx) red grapes
3 large apples
1 pear
Spinach or lettuce leaves
2 large potatoes
6 red onion
9 garlic cloves
2 lime
1 lemon
20g coriander
15g parsley
Optional: red chilli or pickled jalapeños (garnish)
750mL milk of choice
4 Tbs live strained yogurt
100g grated cheddar
850g (approx) chicken legs and thighs (skin on & bone in)
50g chorizo
1 tin of chickpeas

1 tin of mixed beans
1 tin of black beans
1 tin of black eyed beans
1 tin butter beans
2 tins of tomatoes
200g oats
200g basmati rice
150g orzo
8 large tortillas
5 Tbs tahini
40g mixed nuts
40g mixed seeds
40g chia seeds
6 Tbs EVOO
7 Tbs vegetable oil
7 Tbs apple cider vinegar
4 Tbs chipotle paste
1 tsp miso
2 vegetable stock cube
2 Tbs ras-el-hanout
3 Tbs ground cinnamon
1 Tbs smoked paprika
3 Tbs ground cumin
1 Tbs ground coriander
1 Tbs dried oregano
5 tsp sugar
Sea salt
Black pepper
200g frozen corn kernel

MY EXTRA TIPS

Forming new habits is key. When you're looking to add more plants to your diet, thinking you have to change everything you cook can seem overwhelming. Instead, I like to form new habits by making small changes to what I'm already doing. Suddenly it seems easier and automatic. A big thing is fighting the guilty mindset that often surrounds food, just try your best and enjoy what you eat. Here are a few things I do that may help you too:

1. Buy mixes that already provide you with a variety and can easily be added to meals: mixed nuts, mixed seeds, mixed beans, mixed frozen veg/fruit.
2. Add your favourite herbs and spices to everything: a sprinkle of oregano, fennel seeds, thyme, cumin, garam masala, ras-el-hanout these are the ones I always have on hand in the cupboard. Form a habit of adding them into everything you cook.
3. It's all a question of habit. Instead of topping toast with butter and jam in the morning, why not try spreading with tahini or a nut butter. Then top it with whole fruit or veg depending on your fancy, and you can even finish it with a sprinkle of seeds for extra plants.
    1. Almond butter and apple slices.
    2. Tahini and plum slices.
    3. Tahini and kimchi/sauerkraut (for the bold).
    4. Strained yogurt and figs.
4. Keep frozen veg handy to add to pasta sauces, stews, stir fries, beans, toast toppers for a quick easy veg boost. I find the best ones to be peas, corn, broccoli, sliced peppers and spinach.

5. Practice the "mis en place" and batch cooking mindset. This is how chefs make cooking look easy. I like to batch prep breakfasts and stuff them full of plants so I'm always starting the day as I mean to go on, and it removes any potential for guilt if my lunch happens to be a grilled cheese sandwich I really fancied.
6. Check what's in season, it will be cheaper and higher in nutrients. Think local where possible (with a few exceptions where heat and sun is required to grow). And stock up.
7. Make substitutions. Don't be afraid to swap out ingredients in recipes with more seasonal veg/fruit or ingredients you have on hand. I promise not much can go wrong.
8. Take a step back to think, could I add a bit more colour to my plate, a few more herbs.
9. If you're hungry for more recipes after trying out the ones in this book, check out my website:

https://www.spoonfulfelicity.com/

APPLE CRUMBLE PORRIDGE

 10.5

Ingredients (5 portions):

200g oats
750mL milk of choice
4 tsp sugar
Sea salt

3 large apples
250mL water
2 Tbs ground cinnamon

40g mixed nuts
40g mixed seeds (I use sunflower, pumpkin, hemp, and linseed)
40g chia seeds
2 tsp EVOO
1 tsp ground cinnamon

HAPPY

Cinnamon, nuts and berries all contain micronutrients that we're often deficient in and that are needed by every cell in the body and brain to do their job.

FOCUS

Oats contain choline, the precursor needed to make the neurotransmitter called acetyl choline which is needed for memory function and is also the neurotransmitter for the parasympathetic nervous system that keeps us calm and composed.
The sugars in oats are released slowly, making them ideal for blood-sugar control and a great help with weight loss as they slow the arrival of lunch-time hunger pangs.

Method:

The night before/ weekend prep:
1. Mix together 120g oats with 4 tsp sugar and 4 pinches of sea salt. Store in an airtight container to use every morning.
2. Remove the core of the apple and dice them up roughly. Add to a saucepan with the water and cinnamon. Bring to a simmer, stir to distribute the cinnamon evenly, cover with a lid, reduce the heat down to low and leave for 40-50 minutes. The apples should soften into a compote consistency. Transfer to an airtight container and store in the fridge once cooled.
3. Roughly chop the mixed nuts.
4. Heat up the EVOO in a pan, add the nuts, mixed seeds, the remaining 40g of oats and ground cinnamon. Cook on medium heat for 2 minutes or until you can see the oats have turned golden. Add the chia seeds and transfer onto a piece of kitchen paper. Leave to cool then store in an airtight container.

Each morning:
1. Measure out 1 espresso cup (or egg cup) of the porridge mix with 2 espresso cups of milk (approx 150mL). Cook in the microwave for 2 minutes, stirring if required.
2. Top the porridge with 1/5 of the apple mixture and 1/5 of the crumble nut mix.
3. Tuck in.

> Cinnamon protects against hypertension, diabetes and neurodegenerative diseases in controlled experiments.

BERRY PARFAIT OVERNIGHT OATS

Ingredients (4 portions):

120g oats
320mL milk of choice
8 Tbs yogurt (preferably strained with live cultures)
4 Tbs chia seeds, heaped
2 Tbs honey (or you can use caster sugar or any jam)
Sea salt

320g frozen mixed berries (I use a mix of strawberries, raspberries, blackberries, blackcurrant and redcurrant)
30g mixed seeds (I use sunflower, pumpkin, hemp, and linseed)
30g walnuts or almonds

HAPPY

Berries are high in folate which is linked to our levels of serotonin, one of our good mood hormones involved in part in mood regulation. They are also a source of vitamin C which is required to convert dopamine into noradrenaline for an energy boost. Along with oats, they supply us with prebiotic fibre to feed our gut bacteria which reward us with lots of benefits including the production of tryptophan, precursor to serotonin.

Raspberry leaf tea was used by Native Americans to ease birth pains.

Strawberries are on all missions to space as a source of anthocyanins and a smell of home!

Method:

1. In a large bowl: mix together the oats, milk, yogurt, chia seeds, pinch of salt and 1 Tbs honey. Stir vigorously.
2. Defrost the berries in the microwave on full power for 3 minutes. Then stir in the other Tbs of honey. Taste to make sure it's sweet enough for your preference.
3. Roughly chop the nuts and mix them with the seeds in a separate bowl.
4. At this stage you can either store your oat mix and berries in separate airtight containers or layer them up in jars to keep in the fridge, I use empty jam jars to do this so I can easily transport them to work.
5. Either way, layer in your container 2 Tbs overnight oats, then 2 Tbs berries, repeat a second time and finish off with a layer of nuts/seeds.
6. That's a delicious breakfast sorted for the next 4 days.

Feel free to replace the nuts or only use seeds. You can also get creative with the fruits you use.
I like using strained yogurt as it is naturally high in protein and use brands that still contain live cultures for probiotics.

> Berries are known for being an excellent source of anthocyanins and polyphenols. These give them their beautiful colours and have many beneficial health properties including anti-inflammatory, supporting cognition and focus, reducing the risk of diabetes, cardiovascular diseases, certain types of cancer and neurodegenerative diseases such as Alzheimers.

AUTUMN LUNCH BOX

Ingredients (4 portions):

1 tin of chickpeas
1/2 cabbage
1/2 celeriac
2 red onions
1 aubergine
1 pear

1/2 butternut squash
2 Tbs ras-el-hanout
2 tsp cumin
1 tsp cinnamon
4 Tbs vegetable oil
4 Tbs tahini

4 Tbs water
1 lemon
Spinach or lettuce leaves
Sea salt
Black pepper

Make this your own over the season by swapping bits out, I recommend trying it with Brussel sprouts, sweet potato/pumpkin, apple/grape and frozen broccoli.
If you don't enjoy sweet & savoury, feel free to leave the pear out.

Focus

Here's why I think this is the perfect lunch box to bring to work:
- Chickpeas have a low glycemic index and release energy slowly so you're fuelled for the rest of the afternoon;
- Aubergines contain nasunin which dilates blood vessels to lower blood pressure, in case it happens to be a stressful day;
- Cabbage and celeriac are a source of folate which is linked to serotonin levels;
- It's simply delicious!

Pear is a source of manganese which is required for brain signalling. Not sure this is the reason, but pear and rose was Marie Antoinette's favourite juice.

Method:

1. Preheat the oven at 190°C.
2. Peel the onions, halve them and cut each half into quarters.
3. Peel the celeriac by cutting it in half, laying it out flat side down, cutting off both ends and starting in the middle following the edge with the knife to remove the skin. Alternatively, you can leave the skin on if it's easy to clean.
4. Dice the celeriac, cabbage and aubergine into bitesized pieces.
5. Halve and core the pear, then slice into wedges. Do the same with the butternut squash.
6. Drain and rinse the chickpeas, then dry them out by laying them out on a clean tea towel.
7. Place the onions, aubergine, cabbage and celeriac into a roasting tray. Add 2 Tbs vegetable oil, sea salt and the ras-el-hanout. Mix until evenly coated and place in the oven for 50 minutes, giving the vegetables a shake half way through.
8. Lay out the squash and pear wedges on an oiled baking sheet. Sprinkle the cinnamon and some sea salt on top and place in the oven until caramelised all over, approx 40 minutes.
9. Pour the chickpeas onto a baking sheet. Top with the cumin and a drizzle of vegetable oil. Toss until evenly coated and bake for 30 minutes or until crispy.
10. Wash the spinach or lettuce.
11. In a small bowl, add the tahini and lemon juice, whisk into a paste then pour the water in while whisking continuously to form a creamy dressing. Add more water if you desire a runnier texture.
12. Once all the roasted ingredients have cooled down, prepare your lunch boxes: start with a layer of leaves, add the roasted veg and wedges, drizzle the dressing over and finish with a scattering of crispy chickpeas.
13. Sorted, enjoy! I love this one packed up for easy lunches.

> Butternut squash gets its name from it's nutty flavour and buttery texture! Great marketing example there.

MISO TOFU AND AUBERGINE BOWLS

7.5

Ingredients (2 portions):

250g tofu
1 aubergine
100g rice
5g sesame seeds
2 small sweet potatoes (200g)
2 spring onions
Coriander and lime for garnishing

Marinade:
2 Tbs white miso paste
3 Tbs soy sauce
4 Tbs apple cider vinegar
1 grated garlic clove
5g grated ginger
2 tsp sugar

Many dishes around the world praise the aubergine. In France, it's referred to as caviar; an Ottoman aubergine dish is called 'the Imam fainted' due to the effect caused by its deliciousness. It wasn't love at first sight for many cultures though, due to its colour and nightshade cousin.

Aubergines are technically a berry!

CALM

Aubergine skin contains a type of anthocyanins known as delphinidin and its derivative nasunin which lower blood pressure by dilating blood vessels.
It's also rich in prebiotic polyphenols which feed the gut bacteria which can produce tryptophan, the precursor of our serene hormone: serotonin.

Method:

The night before:
1. Place the tofu in between pieces of kitchen roll in a deep container. Place a heavy dish on top of the tofu, and weigh it down further if possible with books. Leave it for 30 minutes.
2. Mix all the marinade ingredients in a bowl.
3. Slice the aubergine into wedges: cut them into quarters, then cut each quarter in 4.
4. Remove the tofu from it's pressing contraption, dry it off and slice into inch-thick slices.
5. Coat everything in the marinade then leave in the fridge overnight.

The evening of:
1. Preheat the oven at 200°C
2. If you want extra tasty rice, rinse it thoroughly. I recommend covering it in cold water, whisking it, then pouring out the water and repeating this process 4 times. Then cover the rice with water and leave to soak.
3. Oil a deep ovenproof dish and tightly pack the aubergine wedges inside. Place in the oven for 30 minutes.
4. In the meantime, cover a baking sheet with parchment paper and lay the tofu slices out flat.
5. Sprinkle sesame seeds over half of each tofu slice.
6. Take the aubergines out and give them a shake, then place them back in the oven along with the tofu slices for another 30 minutes.
7. Thinly slice the spring onions on a bias.
8. Cut the coriander roughly for garnishing.
9. Wash the sweet potatoes and slice them into 2cm-thick circles. Place them in a saucepan, covered with cold water. Bring the pan to a boil, add a pinch of salt, then turn down to a simmer and cook for 8 minutes or until a knife can easily be inserted into them. Drain them and keep to the side for serving.
10. Drain the rice, then put it in a saucepan with 180g of water. Bring to the boil, add a pinch of salt and stir, then transfer to a low heat. Cover the pan and cook for 5 minutes. Finally, remove the lid and cook for a further 5 minutes on a low heat.
11. Fluff up the rice with a fork.
12. Layer everything up in a bowl, garnish with a bit of coriander and 1/2 lime. Enjoy!

PARSLEY PESTO PASTA

2.5

Ingredients (4 portions):

80g almonds
80g parsley
60g grana padano
80mL EVOO

2 small garlic cloves
Sea salt
Black Pepper
360g pasta

I love pesto because it so easy and versatile. You can switch up the nuts, herb, cheese for anything you have on hand. Parsley also goes really nicely with cheddar, I also love the combination of kale or cabbage leaves parboiled and mixed with walnuts.

HAPPY

Parsley is a source of iron, calcium, potassium, folate, vitamin C and vitamin K which whole play a role in our good mood:
Low levels of iron are linked to lethargy and feeling weak;
Folate and calcium are required to convert tryptophan to serotonin;
Vitamin C is required to convert dopamine to noradrenaline (runner's high? More like pesto high!);
Vitamin K intake has been linked to lowered depressive symptoms in early studies.

EVOO is a great source of polyphenols and some research links it to improved cognition.

Method:

1. Warm the almonds in a dry frying pan on medium heat for 2-3 minutes or until they start to brown.
2. Add the almonds, garlic, grana padano and EVOO to a food processor and blitz to a paste. Add the parsley (stems and all), pinch of salt and black pepper to the food processor and blitz again. Adjust seasoning to taste if needed.
3. Cook your pasta of choice until al dente in salted boiling water. Reserve some pasta water and add to the food processor to loosen the pesto up if needed.
4. Stir the pesto into the pasta with extra pasta water until the sauce evenly coats the pasta. The pasta water will melt the cheese and help it emulsify into a silky sauce.
5. Serve up 2 portions and save the other 2 for tomorrow's lunch.
6. Enjoy one of my favourite meals, bon appétit!

> Parsley is a great support to eye health as it contains vitamin A precursors.

> If you have enough of it, there's not much parsley can't do. I could write a poem to my admiration of parsley! I won't though don't worry…
> But bear in mind it's a source of fibre, vitamins A, B1, B7, B9, C, E, K, iron, potassium and calcium!

MOROCCAN INSPIRED CHICKPEA STEW

15.5

Ingredients (4 portions):

200g potatoes
1 tin of chickpeas
1 red onion
1 pepper
1 carrot
250g seasonal cabbage (approx 2/3)
1/2 leek
1 tin of tomatoes
100g spinach
30g rocket
35g dried apricots (approx 5)
2 garlic cloves
2 tsp harissa paste
2 tsp ground cumin
2 tsp ras-el-hanout
1 tsp ground cinnamon
1 lemon
1 Tbs EVOO
20g flaked almonds
8g coriander
8g parsley
2 Tbs yogurt (strained with live cultures)

HAPPY

Spinach is a source of iron and calcium (also found in the yogurt) which is involved in the conversion cycle of tryptophan to serotonin, one of our good mood hormones.

This dish is also high in vitamin C from the parsley, spinach and peppers which not only supports iron absorption, but also the conversion of dopamine to noradrenaline for a good mood boost.

The smell that a lot of people hate in cabbage is due to sulfur based compounds called glucosinolates, these have actually been shown to have protective effects against certain types of cancers, so embrace the stink!

Popeye the sailor man's love of spinach increased sales by 30% in the US!

Method:

1. Peel the onion and carrot. Dice the onion into small pieces.
2. Cut the leeks in half lengthways then run them under cold water making sure to wash between each leaf. Shake off the excess water then slice very thinly.
3. In a large saucepan, add 1 Tbs oil and heat it up on medium. When warm, add the leeks and onion and leave to sweat for 5 minutes or until they start to brown slightly.
4. In the meantime, peel the carrot and chop both the potatoes and carrots into 2-inch sized chunks.
5. Remove the stem of the pepper and slice it into strips.
6. Remove the core of the cabbage and roughly chop it into 1-inch sized pieces.
7. Slice a whole lemon into thin slices and roughly chop the dried apricots into small pieces.
8. Add the cumin, ras-el-hanout, cinnamon and crushed garlic cloves to the pan, stir and leave to warm through for 1 minute. Add the lemon and harissa paste then stir that through.
9. Add all the other vegetables to the pan, along with the drained chickpeas, tin of tomatoes and 1/2 tin's worth of water. Bring to the boil, then stir and reduce the heat to low before covering and leaving to slowly simmer for 30 minutes.
10. Prepare the garnishes. Toast the almond flakes in a dry pan for 2 minutes or until slightly golden.
11. Roughly chop the coriander and parsley then stir it through the yogurt in a small bowl.
12. Mix 2 tsp EVOO with 1 tsp harissa to create a spicy drizzle.
13. Once the stew has been simmering away for 30 minutes, check the potatoes are cooked by inserting the tip of a knife in them. If so, serve up in a bowl with a dollop of herby yogurt, sprinkle of almonds and drizzle of harissa oil.

Note: any leftovers can be frozen for 3 months to have on hand. Feel free to make this your own adding different vegetables like butternut squash, kale, celeriac, or anything else you fancy!

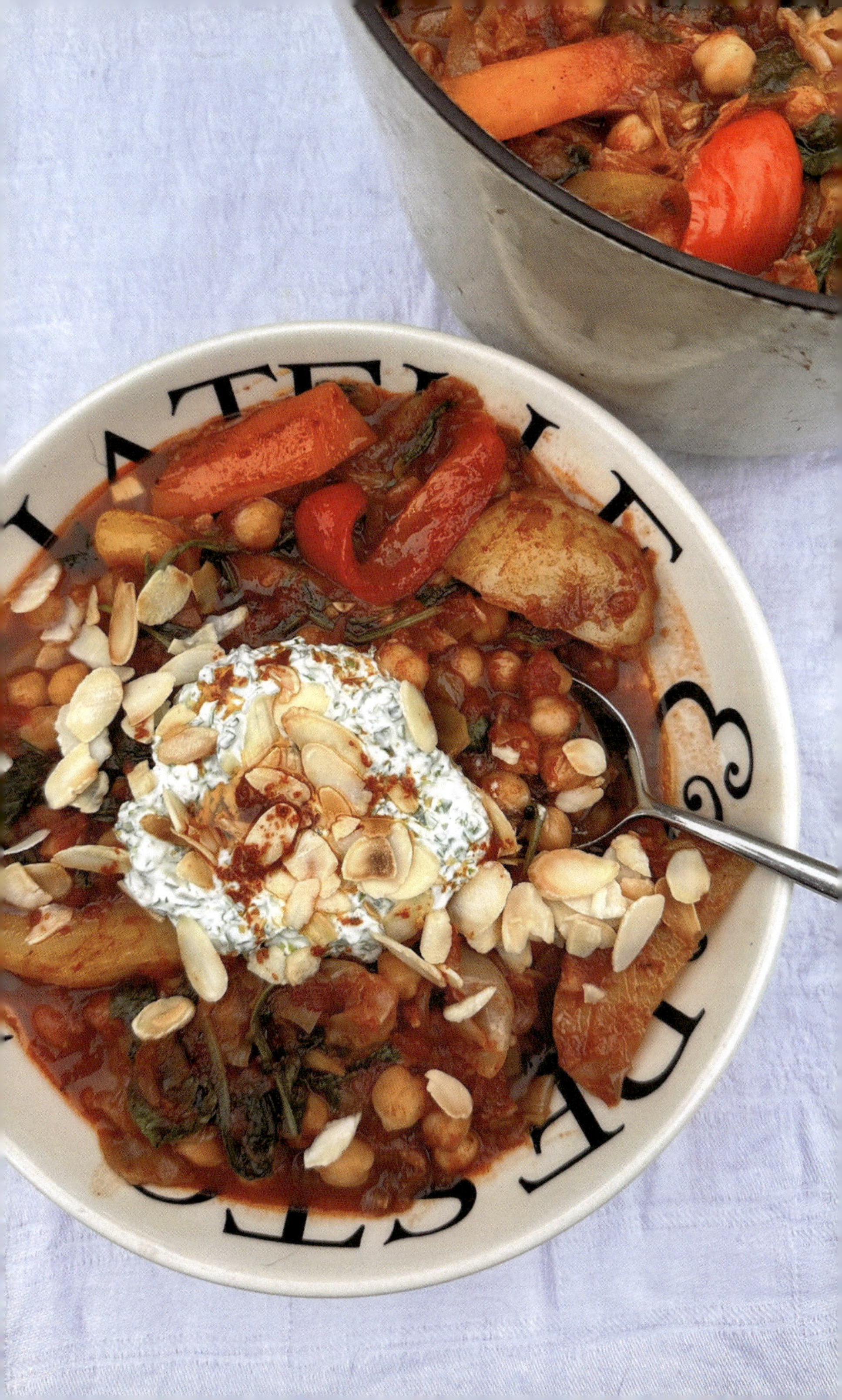

CHICKEN, LEEK & MUSHROOM PIE

8.25

Do not hesitate to make substitutes as always. Use double the amount of dijon (or English) instead of wholegrain mustard, and swap out the vegetables for anything you have: corn, carrots, peppers, different greens.

Ingredients (4 portions):

300g button mushrooms
2 chicken breasts
1 tin of green lentils
1/2 leek
1/3 seasonal cabbage
100g frozen broccoli
80g frozen peas
2 garlic cloves
1 vegetable stock cube
25g plain flour
250mL water
250mL milk

1 tsp dijon mustard
1 tsp wholegrain mustard
35g parsley
5 sheets of filo pastry
4 Tbs EVOO
2 tsp balsamic vinegar
10g grana padano cheese
Sea salt and black pepper

Optional:
1tsp marmite
Worcestershire sauce

HAPPY

Chicken is high in protein and especially the amino acid tryptophan, which is the precursor to the good mood hormone serotonin, required for mood regulation and a feeling of serene happiness. Leeks are rich in folate which is also linked to levels of serotonin. They are also high in vitamin C which is required to convert dopamine to noradrenaline.

Leeks are the symbol of Wales as they were used to distinguish the Welsh from the Saxons in the battle of 640 AD. They became a symbol of health and virtue and many girls believed sleeping with one under their pillow would allow them to see their future husband in their dreams.

Peas and Leeks were both eaten at least 5,000 years ago!

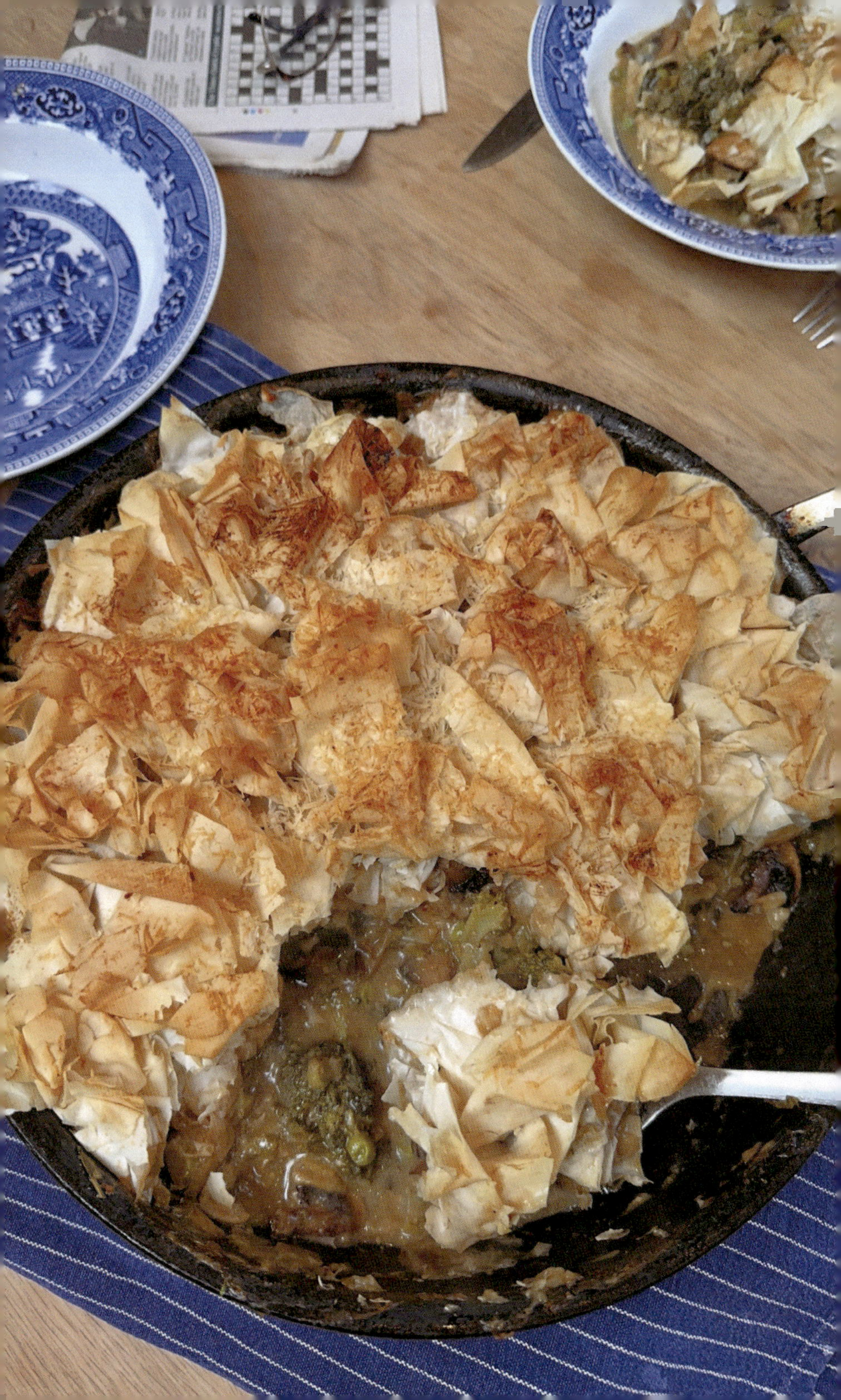

Method:
1. Preheat the oven at 200°C.
2. Scrub the mushrooms with a dry sponge to remove any dirt. Then cut them into quarters. Brown then on medium heat for 10 minutes in an ovenproof pan.
3. In the meantime, cut the chicken up into 2-inch cubes.
4. On a separate chopping board, slice washed leeks very thinly.
5. Remove the core of the cabbage and dice it into 1-inch pieces.
6. Peel the garlic cloves and slice thinly.
7. Transfer the browned mushrooms onto a plate, then add 1 Tbs oil to the pan. Add the chicken and cook for 3 minutes on both side or until browned all over.
8. Transfer the chicken onto the mushroom plate. Reduce the heat of the pan to low, add 1 Tbs oil and the garlic slices. Leave to sizzle in the oil for 30 seconds then add the leeks with a pinch of salt. Sweat them off stirring occasionally for 4 minutes.
9. Add the cabbage, frozen broccoli florets and another pinch of salt then leave to cook for 6 minutes.
10. Boil water in the kettle and roughly chop the parsley.
11. Add the flour to the pan and stir it until it coats all the ingredients. Add the milk and stir it in, then add the boiling water and veg stock cube. Stir it on a simmer until it thickens then remove from the heat. Add in the mustard and a crack of black pepper. If you have it in the cupboard, also add 1 tsp marmite and a few dashes of Worcestershire sauce.
12. Add the frozen peas, drained lentils, chopped parsley, chicken and mushroom and stir them in until everything is evenly coated in the sauce.
13. In a small bowl, mix 2 Tbs EVOO with 2 tsp balsamic vinegar. Rub a bit onto both sides of a sheet of filo pastry with a pastry brush. Tear up the sheet of filo in 2 then scrunch the pieces up and place them onto the filling. Repeat this until the whole pan in covered in scrunched up filo.
14. Grate the cheese onto the pastry, then bake in the oven until golden, about 20 minutes.
15. Serve up and enjoy while it's hot! You can freeze any leftover portions to have at another time.

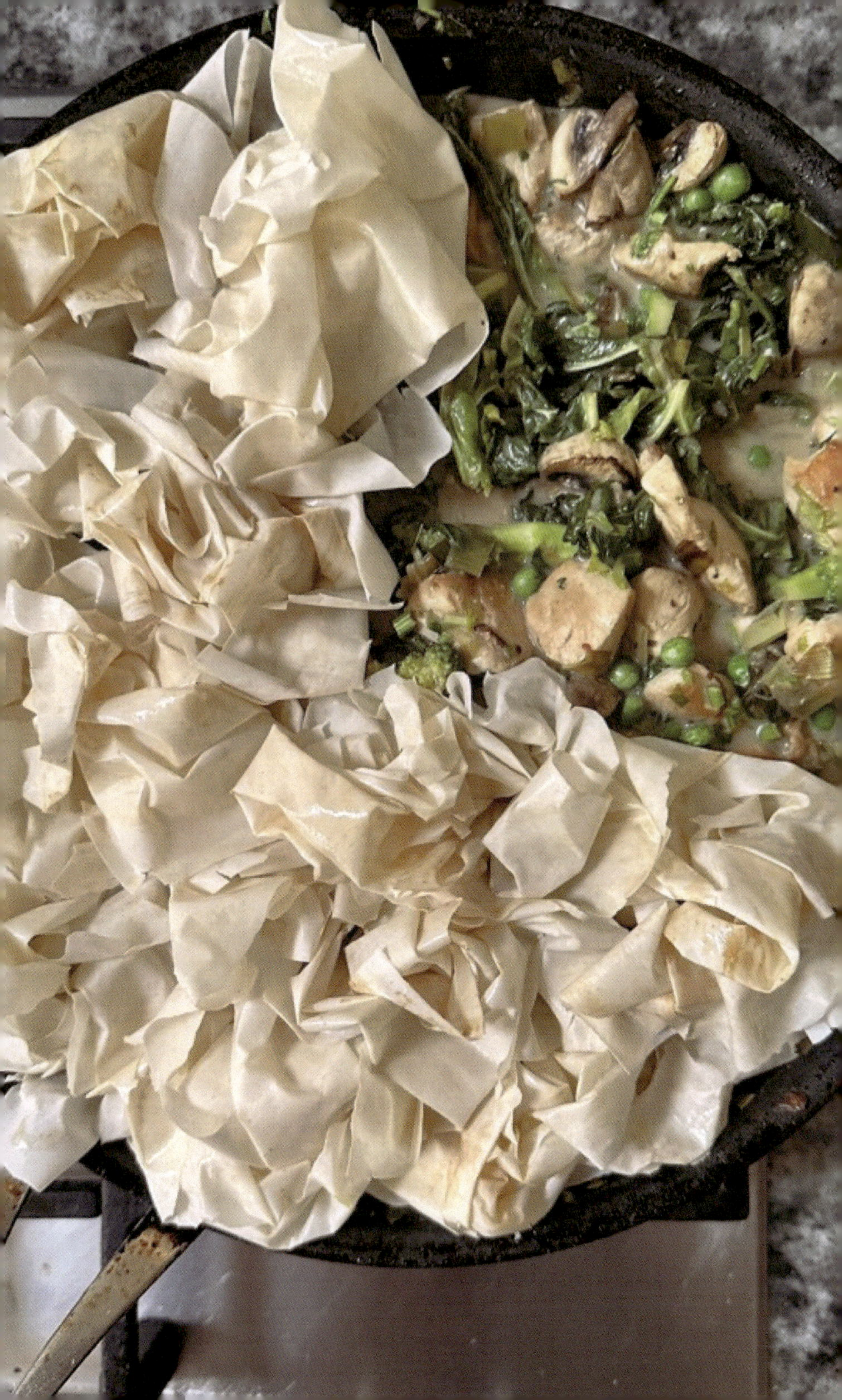

5 BEAN CHILLI BURRITO BOWL

18

Fo me, this chilli is the ultimate batch cooking recipe. It stores very well in the freezer and can be turned into different meals such as my burrito bowl or quesadillas. Make it your own by switching up the vegetables.

5 Bean Chilli Ingredients (8 portions):

1 tin of mixed beans
1 tin of black beans
1 tin of black eyed beans
2 red onions
2 carrots
2 celery sticks
3 red peppers
200g frozen corn kernels
2 tins of tomatoes

2 Tbs vegetable oil
1 vegetable stock cube
1 Tbs smoked paprika
2 Tbs ground cumin
1 Tbs ground coriander
1 Tbs dried oregano
1 tsp ground cinnamon
3 Tbs chipotle paste
Sea salt

Burrito Bowl Ingredients (4 portions):

200g basmati rice
250mL water
1/2 red onion
1 carrot
1/3 cucumber
100g seasonal cabbage
50g spinach
7g coriander
1 lime
4 Tbs apple cider vinegar

1 tsp chipotle paste
Sea salt and black pepper
4 Tbs yogurt (preferably one with live cultures)
Optional: red chilli or pickled jalapeños (garnish)

HAPPY

Peppers are rich in folate which is linked to levels of serotonin, a hormone required for mood regulation. They are also high in vitamin C which is required to convert dopamine to noradrenaline.

Peppers have been eaten for 9,000 years.

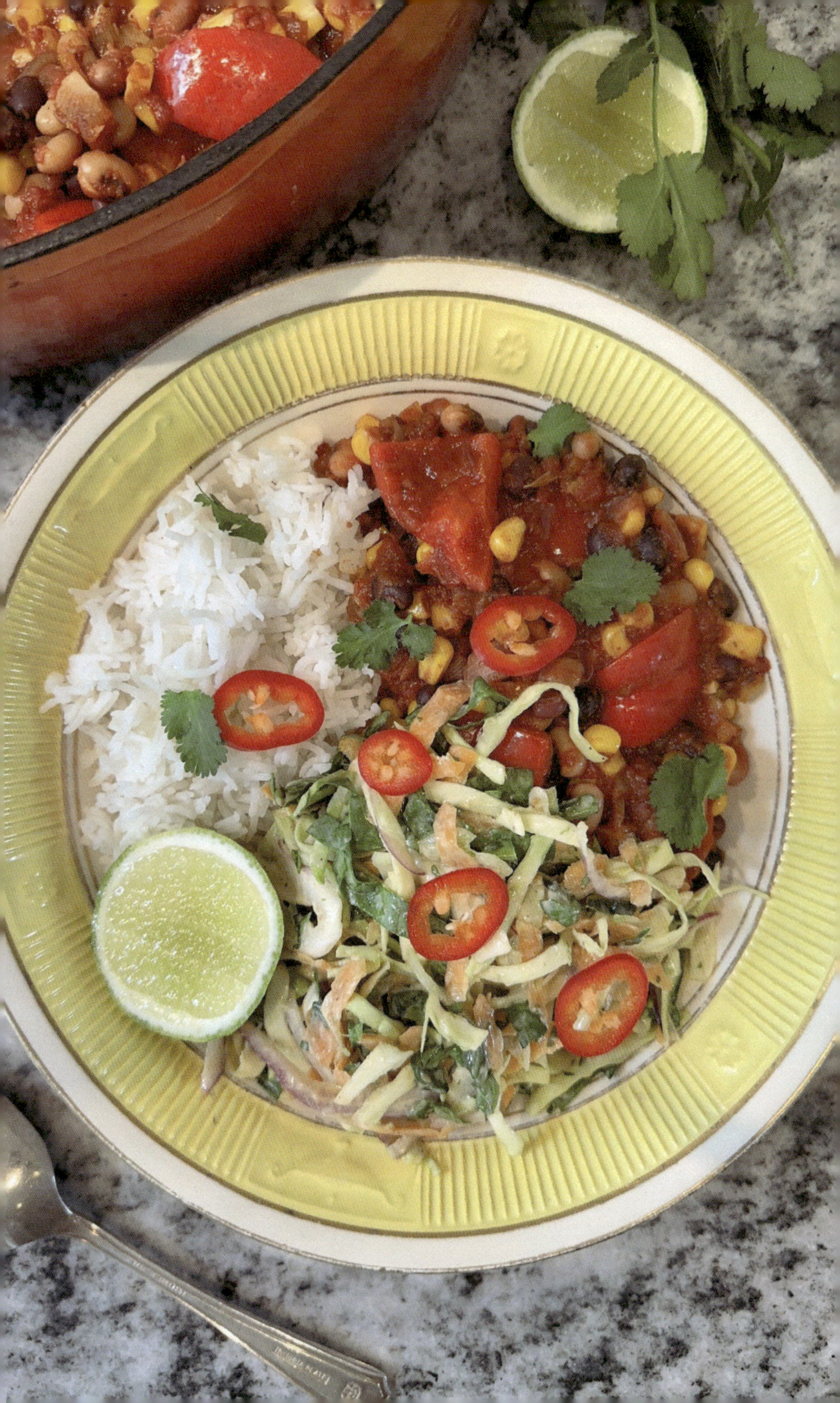

Method:

Chilli Batch Cooking:
1. This recipe starts with a lot of veg chopping. That's why I like to make a big batch when I have more time at the weekend, so it can be used in other recipes throughout the week or kept in the freezer for 3 months to have on hand.
2. Peel and dice in small pieces the red onions, carrots and celery sticks.
3. Warm up 2 Tbs vegetable oil in a large saucepan on a medium heat. Transfer the onion, carrot and celery to the saucepan and leave to sweat. Stir occasionally and reduce the heat if it starts browning too much.
4. Roughly chop the peppers into large chunks, removing the stem in the process.
5. Once the veg in the saucepan have started to brown slightly and soften (approx 5 minutes), add the dried spices and stir them in for 1 minute. Then add the chipotle paste and stir this in.
6. Add the peppers, corn kernels and drained beans. Stir everything in until it's all evenly distributed. Then add the veg stock cube, the 2 tins of tomatoes and 1 tin's worth of water.
7. Bring the mix to a boil then stir and reduce down to the lowest heat before covering with a lid and leaving to gently simmer for 30 minutes.

> 1 red pepper contains more than our daily required dose of vitamin C. Make room in the limelight oranges!

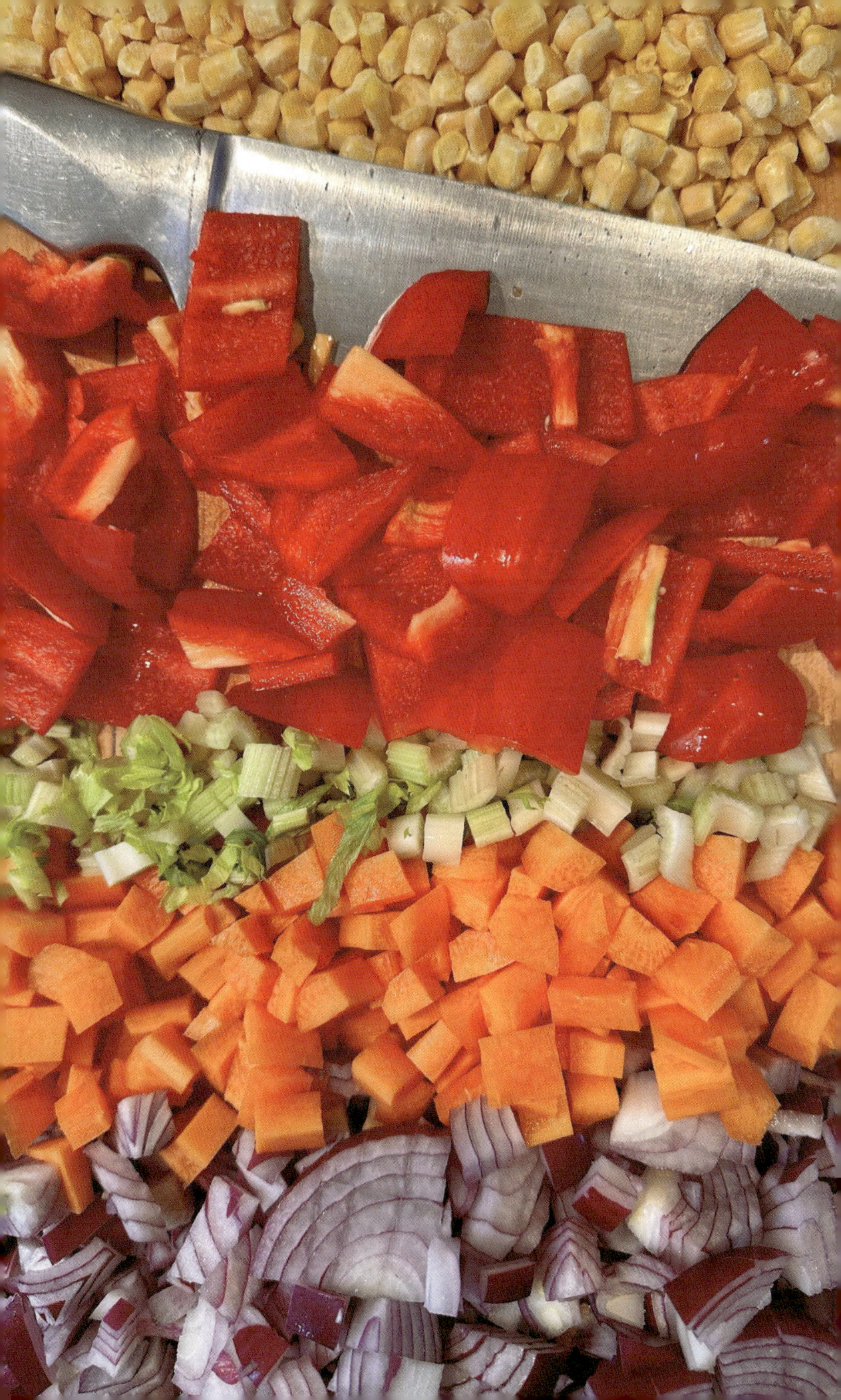

Burrito Bowl Method:

1. Prepare the rice: rinse it 6 times with cold water then cover with water and leave to soak while you prepare the coleslaw.
2. Peel the red onion and carrot.
3. Grate the carrot and cucumber into a large bowl.
4. Thinly slice the red onion, cabbage and spinach leaves as thinly as you can, then add them to the bowl.
5. Roughly chop the coriander, using a back and forth motion with the knife.
6. Add the coriander, apple cider vinegar, chipotle paste and a generous amount of salt and pepper to the slaw.
7. Scrunch up all the veg with your hands to break them down a bit. Then add the yogurt and stir it in. Taste to make sure it doesn't need any more salt.

Assembly:

8. Heat the chilli up on medium heat.
9. Prepare the garnishes: thinly slice the red chilli and cut up some lime wedges.
10. Drain the rice then place it in a saucepan with 250mL of water. Bring it to the boil on a high heat, then add a bit of salt and stir it in. Move to a low heat and cover the pan, cook for 5 minutes then remove the lid and cook for a further 5 minutes. Fluff the rice up with a fork.
11. While the rice is cooking, remove the lid from the chili and leave it to reduce until the rice is ready.
12. Serve it all up in a bowl and enjoy with a finishing squeeze of lime juice.

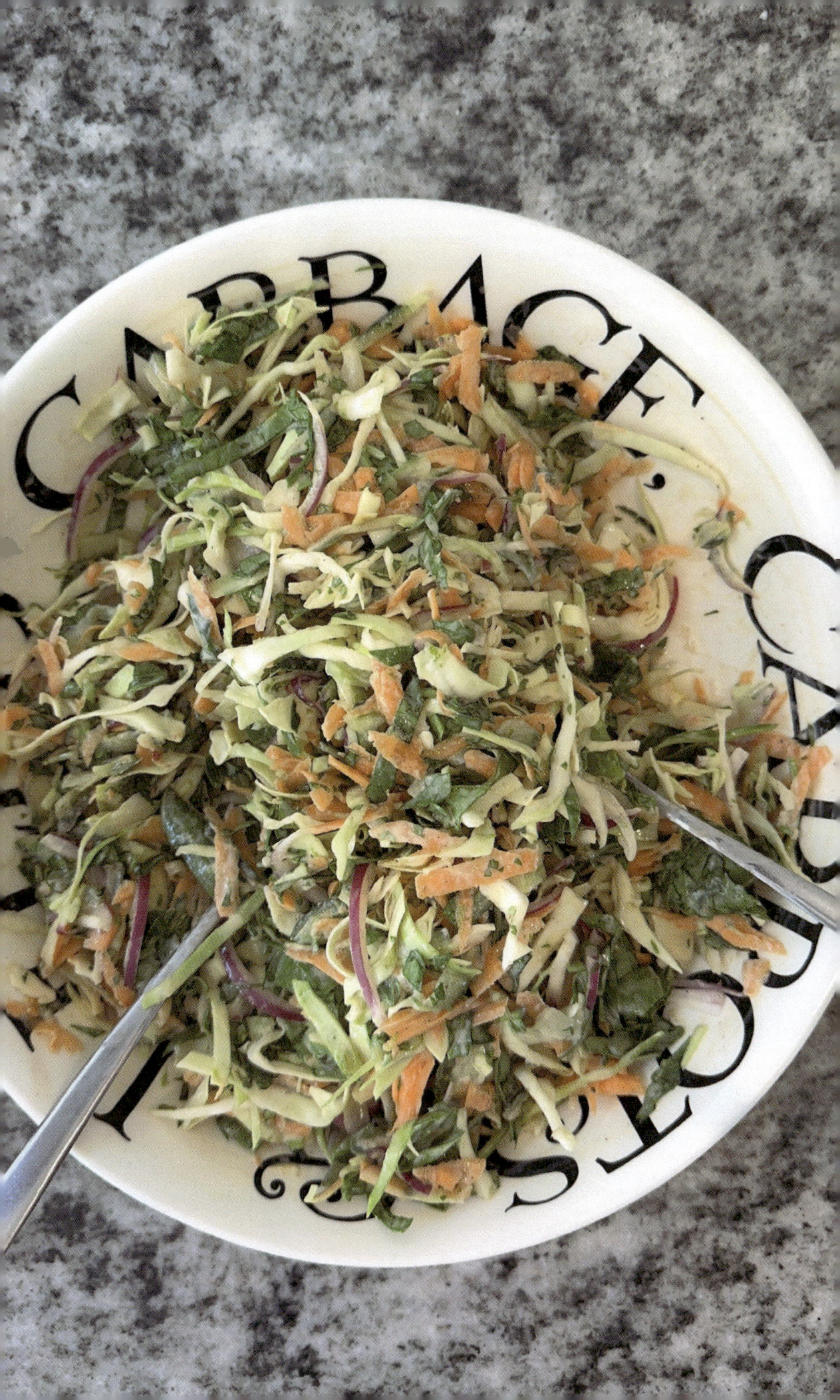
CABBAGE

5 BEAN QUESADILLAS

Ingredients (4 portions):

14.75

300g 5 bean chilli (see previous recipe)
8 large tortillas
100g grated cheddar
12g coriander (garnish)
1 lime

1/2 red onion
2 Tbs apple cider vinegar
1 tsp salt
1 tsp sugar

FOCUS

Corn is a source of B vitamins which support the conversion of food into energy by the body and contribute to higher alertness and concentration. Tiredness can be linked to B vitamin deficiency. It also has a low glycemic index and therefore releases energy from food steadily over a prolonged period.

Some people have olfactory receptors which identify coriander as soap.

Maize (Corn) was cultivated from wild grass in Central America 7,000 years ago. It is now one of the largest worldwide crop production for animal feed, biofuel and food.

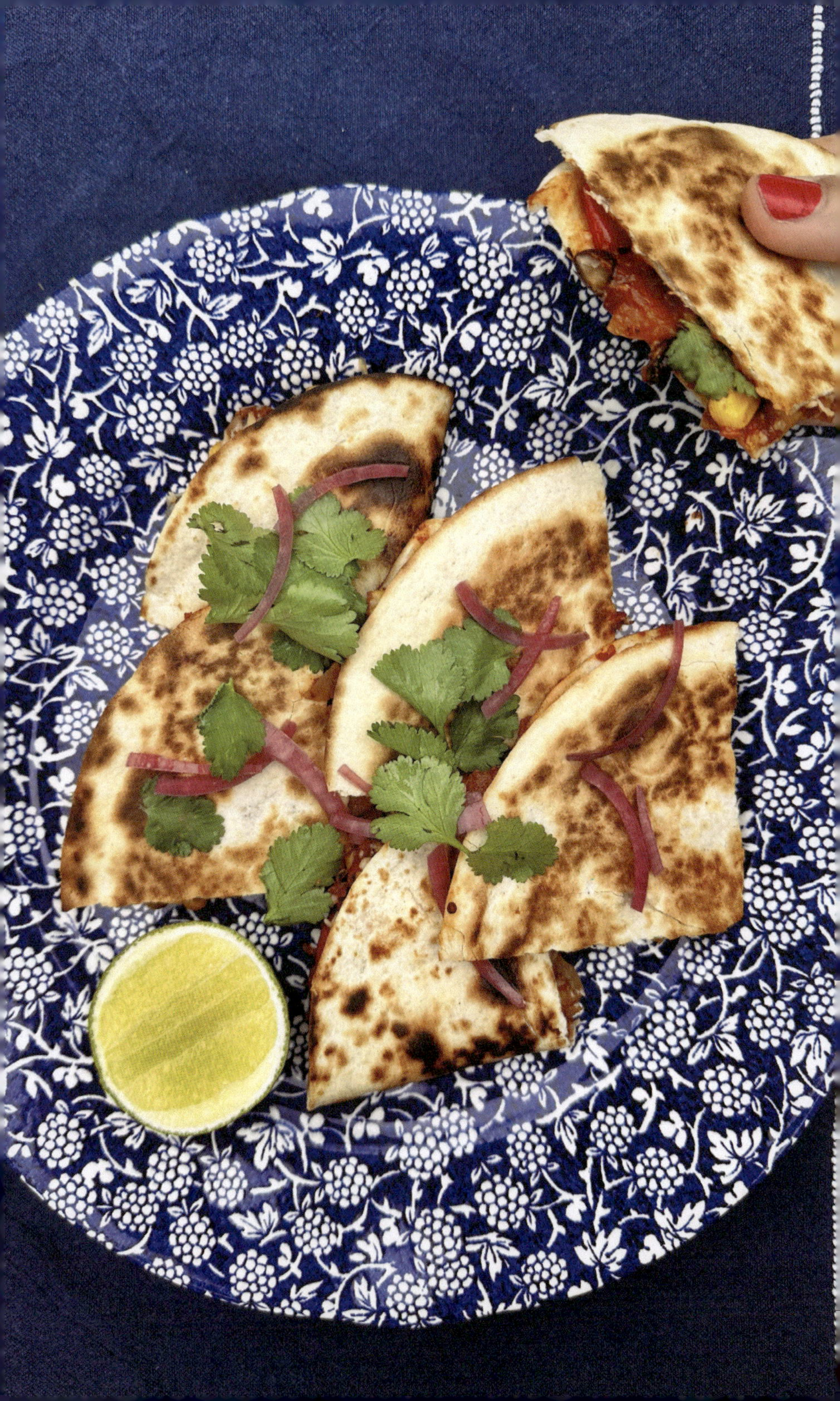

Method:

1. Peel and thinly slice the red onion. Rinse it in cold water and drain.
2. In a bowl, add the red onion, apple cider vinegar, salt and sugar. Scrunch it all up with your hands and leave to sit on the side while you prepare the rest.
3. Grate the cheddar, roughly chop the coriander and cut the lime up into wedges.
4. Warm up a pan on medium heat.
5. Place a tortilla in the pan, add 150g of cold chilli (about 4 Tbs) and 25g of the grated cheddar. Place another tortilla on top.
6. Leave to cook on the pan for 3 minutes or until it starts to brown, then flip over. Cook for another 2 minutes to brown the other side and make sure the cheese has melted.
7. Serve warm with a garnish of pickled red onion, coriander and lime wedge.

> Corn contains lutein and zeaxanthin pigments which support eye health and slow down macular degeneration.

> Combining cereal grains with beans makes them a complete protein with all essential amino acids. Avengers assemble!

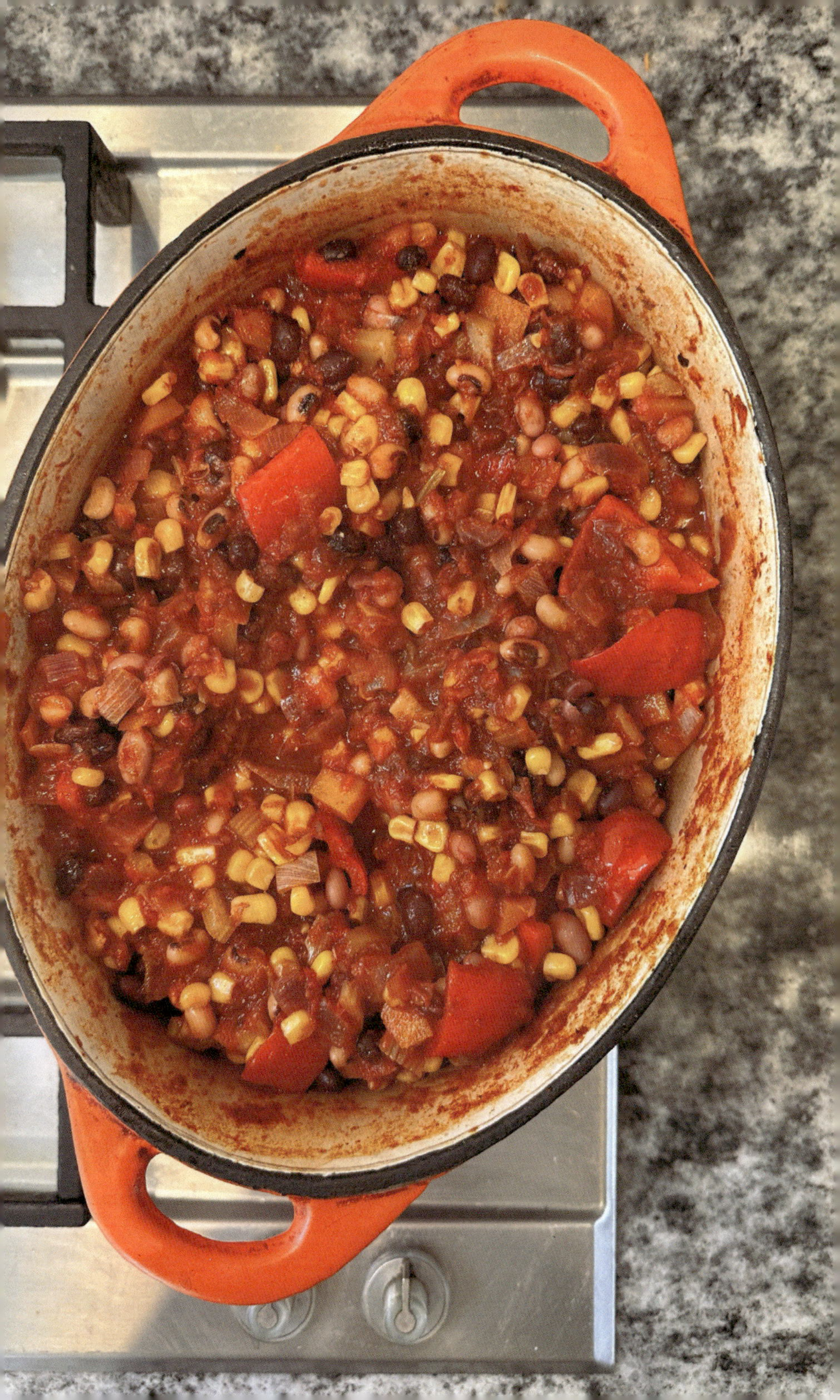

BUTTERNUT SQUASH & CHORIZO ORZOTTO

5.5

Ingredients (2 portions):

500g butternut squash (approx 1/2 large one)
2 garlic cloves
2 Tbs EVOO
1 red onion
1 Tbs vegetable oil
150g orzo
1 veg stock cube

50g chorizo
1 tin butter beans
1 tsp miso
1 Tbs tahini
Sea salt
Smoked paprika
Black pepper

FOCUS

Butternut squash contains a carotenoid pigment called lutein which has anti-inflammatory properties that support cognitive function.
Butter beans have a low glycemic index for a controlled steady release of energy to the brain.
Chorizo is a source of my favourite amino acid: tryptophan, the precursor of serotonin.

Butternut squash seeds and skins are a good source of antioxidants which prevent cardiovascular diseases and certain types of cancer. Why are we throwing that away? Roast them with spices for a tasty snack.

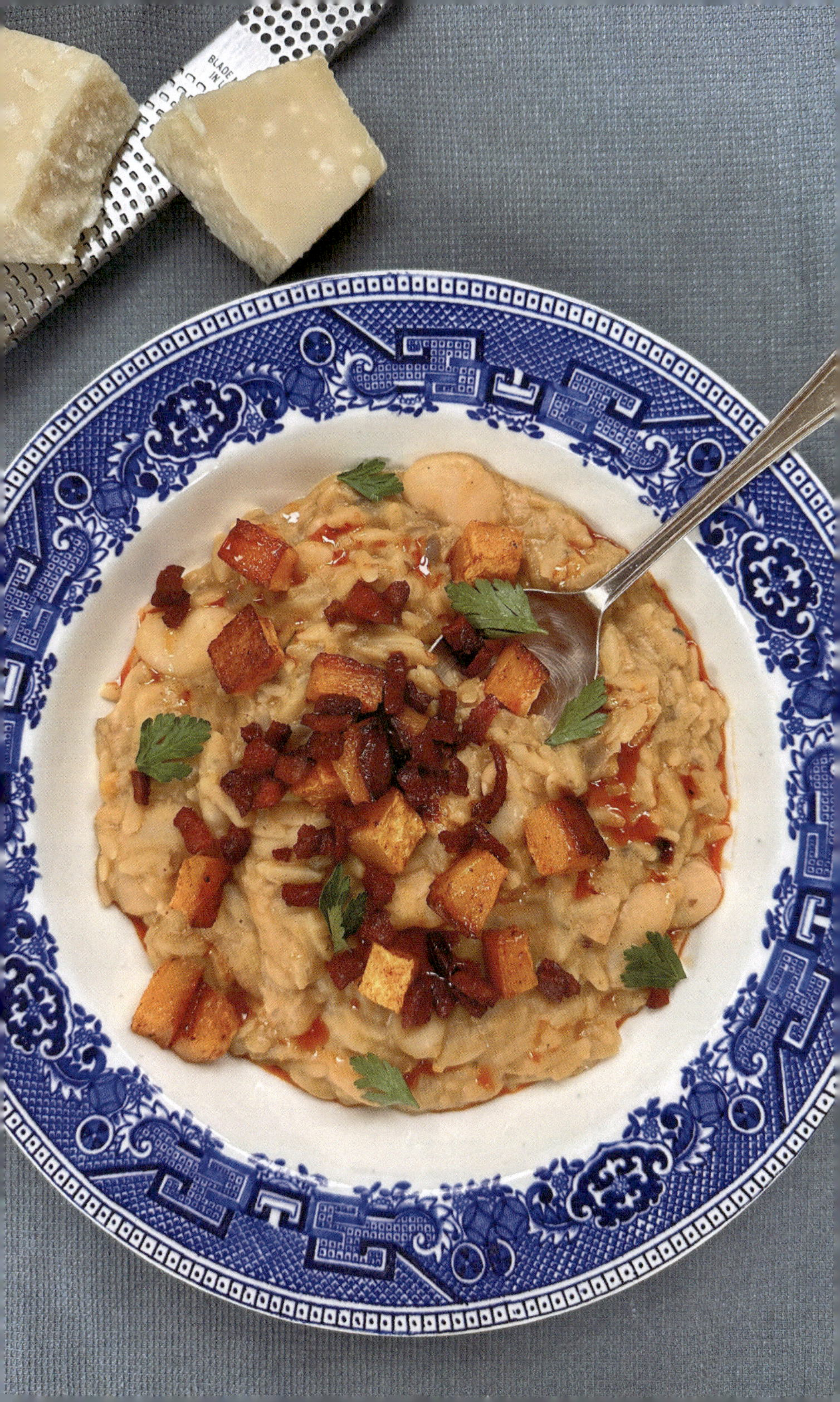

Method:

1. Preheat the oven at 200°C.
2. Dice up the butternut squash, and remove the seeds if needed (depending on which half you're using).
3. Place it on a baking sheet with the oil, garlic cloves, a couple pinches of salt, black pepper and 4 pinches of smoked paprika.
4. Toss it all to coat the butternut squash pieces evenly.
5. Roast in the oven for 40 minutes.
6. After about 15 minutes, peel and dice the red onion into small pieces. Add 1 Tbs vegetable oil to a frying pan on medium heat. Add the red onion and sweat them off for 6 minutes, stirring occasionally.
7. Boil a full kettle of water.
8. Add the orzo to the pan and stir it through the onions for 1 minute.
9. Mix the veg stock cube with 450mL of boiling water, then add to the pan of orzo. Bring back to the boil then turn the heat down to low, add the drained butter beans and cover with a lid. Leave covered to cook for 15 minutes.
10. In the meantime, peel and dice the chorizo, then cook in a dry pan for 4 minutes until browned and crispy, and remove from the heat.
11. When the butternut squash has had 40 minutes, take out the garlic cloves and half of the pieces. Peel the garlic cloves and add them with the butternut squash to a food processor. Leave the rest of the squash pieces in the oven, turned off, to keep warm.
12. Add the miso, tahini and 200mL boiling water to the food processor containing the garlic and butternut then blitz until smooth. Taste and season with salt and pepper as required.
13. Stir this mixture into the orzo.
14. Serve the orzotto into bowls and top off with the remaining butternut squash and chorizo pieces. Dig in while it's hot!

> Butternut squash gets its beautiful colour from carotenoids, in particular beta-carotene, which supports eye health!

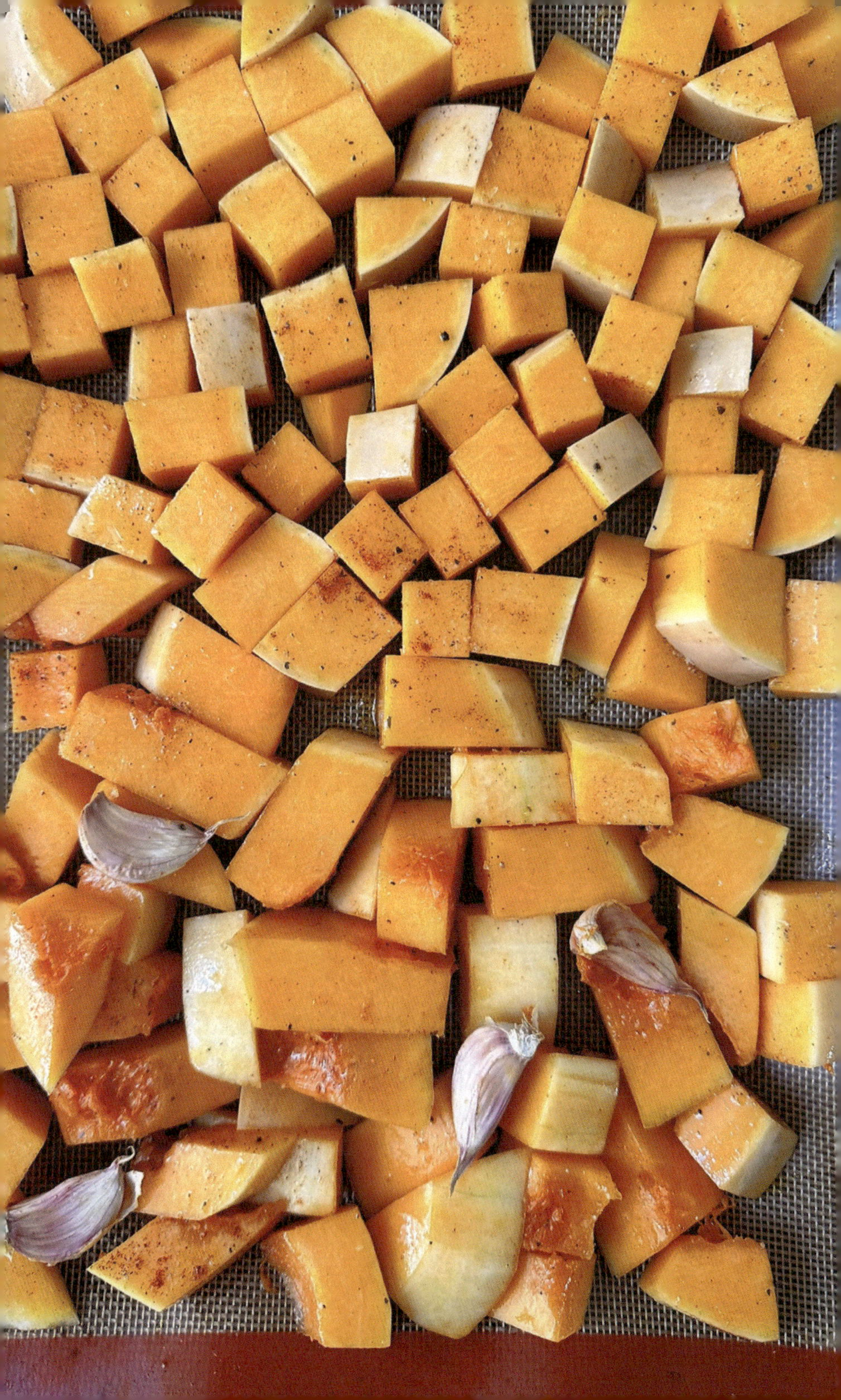

AUTUMN CHICKEN TRAY BAKE

5.75

Ingredients (4 portions):

850g (approx) chicken legs and thighs (skin on & bone in)
1/2 celeriac
2 large potatoes
170g (approx) button mushrooms
240g (approx) red grapes
1/2 cabbage
6 garlic cloves

Sea salt and black pepper
2 Tbs EVOO

Parsley 'chimichurri':
15g parsley
1 tsp EVOO
1 tsp apple cider vinegar
1/2 garlic clove
Sea salt and black pepper

If you don't enjoy sweet & savoury, remove the grape from the recipe, I'm not forcing you!

CALM

Celeriac contains an antioxidant called apigenin which has been shown to lower anxiety and insomnia.
Chicken is a source of amino acids including tryptophan which, you might be bored of me saying this now, is the precursor of our serene happy hormone serotonin.
Red grape is a source of vitamin K which may be inversely linked to depressive symptoms.

Did you know mushrooms can also make vitamin D?
They would love a little tanning session in the South of France!

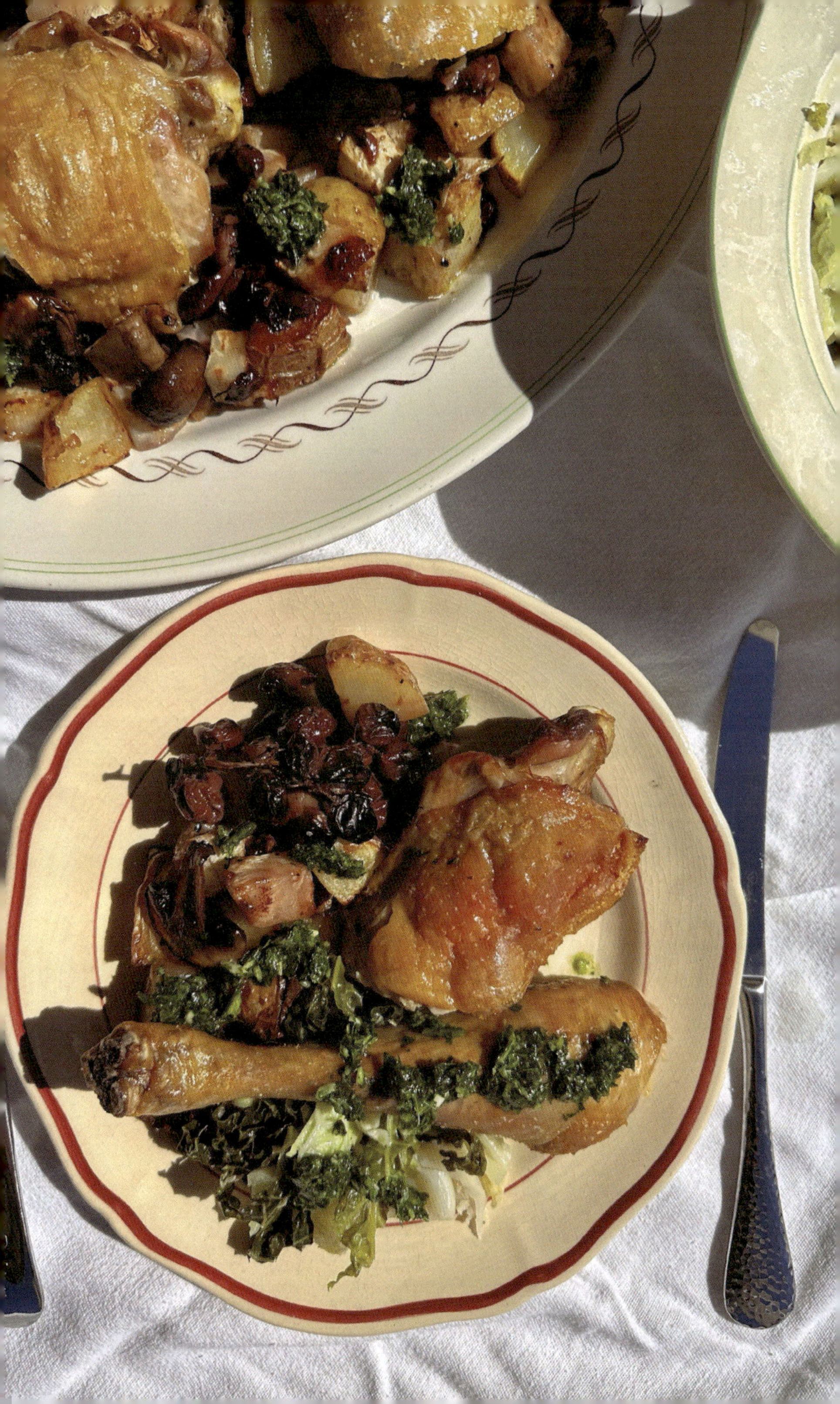

Method:

1. Preheat the oven at 230°C.
2. Clean the mushrooms with a dry sponge and peel the celeriac.
3. Slice the mushrooms in half, and cut the potatoes and celeriac into bitesized pieces.
4. Remove the grape stems, and use the flat side of a knife to smash the garlic cloves.
5. Place all the vegetables, garlic cloves and grapes in a baking tray and toss in the oil, salt and pepper.
6. Season the chicken generously with salt and place on a wire rack on top of the baking tray.
7. Place it all in the oven, reduce the temperature down to 190°C and roast for 40 minutes.
8. Remove the chicken from the oven and leave it to rest on the side for 10 minutes (leave it uncovered to keep the skin crispy).
9. Shake the vegetables up a bit and leave them in the oven to finish cooking while the chicken rests.
10. Remove the core of the cabbage, slice it very thinly and steam for 6 minutes. Dress the cooked cabbage with a drizzle of EVOO or a squeeze of lemon juice.
11. Chop the parsley up finely and mix it with the apple cider vinegar, EVOO, salt and 1/2 a grated raw garlic clove.
12. Drizzle the parsley sauce over the vegetables and serve up 2 portions. Save the other 2 for tomorrow's lunch, bon appétit!

It's the polyphenols (antioxidants) found in red grape skins which some people use to justify that cheeky glass of wine with lunch.

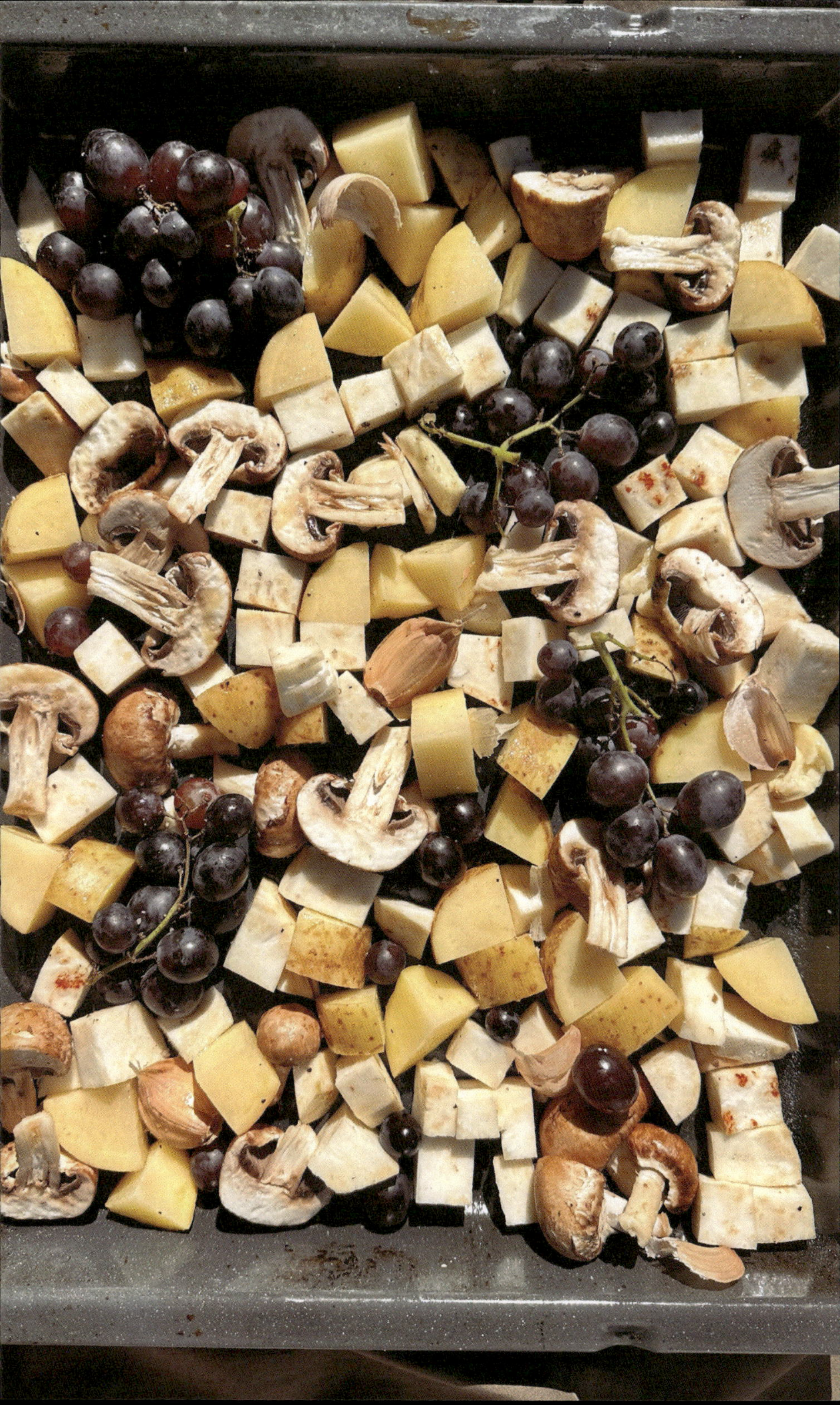

ABOUT THE AUTHOR

My name is Felicity Vincent. Aside from being a woman who loves to cook and eat, I'm a trained chef who worked in several kitchens after graduating from the Cordon Bleu Paris. Just cooking food wasn't enough for me though, I was keen to understand the magic behind the curtain and went on to study Food Science and Nutrition at University of Nottingham. I learnt a lot about what food is made of and how it interacts with our body.

After four years working as a product developer for a blue chip company, I've decided to devote myself to my passion: developing nutritious recipes that help everyone love plants and live a happier lifestyle through delicious food. And bonus, it's better for the planet too!

Printed in Great Britain
by Amazon